our daily tread

thoughts for an inspired life

P9-CDK-374

Copyright © 2008 Aerie River, Inc.
www.aerieriver.com

our daily tread is published by Aerie River Books and
Islandport Press, in collaboration with Wheelock College.
Support for this project was provided by Bowdoin College
alumni, Safe Passage, David DeLorme, Brita H. Bonechi
and Penmor Lithographers.

All rights reserved. No part of this book may be reproduced
in any form or by any electronic or mechanical means,
including information storage and retrieval systems, without
express permission from the publisher.

First Edition

ISBN 978-1-934031-21-6

Library of Congress Control Number:
2008939191

The photographs that appear in **our daily tread** were taken in
and around Guatemala. The artwork was created by children
in Guatemala City who participate in Safe Passage programs.

Picture Credits: Cover photograph, Mike Glad © 2002
Children's artwork © 2007 Safe Passage
All other pictures copyright of photographers as noted:
Joseph Delconzo © 2000, 2002, 2004, 2005, 2006;
Mike Glad © 2002; Antonia Munroe © 2007;
Mike Ritter © 2007; John Santerre © 2002, 2004;
Jon Torres © 2007; and Danielle Torres © 2007

Art direction, design and typesetting: Bonnie Hamalainen

Printed by Penmor Lithographers of Lewiston, Maine
on Forest Stewardship Council (FSC) certified papers using
non-toxic ink.

FSC
Mixed Sources
Product group from well-managed
forests and recycled wood or fiber
Cert no. SW-COC-002383
www.fsc.org
© 1996 Forest Stewardship Council

our daily tread

thoughts for an inspired life

Lisa M. Belisle, M.D., M.P.H., *Editor*

aerie river

BOOKS

our daily tread was created to honor the late Hanley Denning:
Visionary, runner, and founder of Safe Passage.
It is dedicated to her family and the children of her heart.

contents

foreword

our daily tread is a yearlong literary journey across a landscape of profound themes: Live with joy. Live deliberately. Share what you have, and who you are, with others. These themes were the life lessons of our friend, Hanley Denning.

Hanley was a Maine girl. Her parents, Marina and Mike, raised her in Yarmouth, an older sister to Jordan, Seth and Lucas. I met her as a high school student. We both attended the Maine Summer Humanities program as rising seniors, not knowing that we would eventually attend college together at Bowdoin.

Hanley had a ready smile and a slightly goofy sense of humor. Though I later learned that she excelled academically and was a state champion runner while at Greely High School in Cumberland, I would never have guessed this from her unpretentious manner. She enjoyed poring over celebrity magazines and eating chocolate. She lived life with joy.

Hanley also lived deliberately; she understood what she needed to do to be successful. She graduated from Bowdoin in 1992 and earned a graduate degree in education from Wheelock College in 1996. She then became a teacher in North Carolina. Finding herself challenged by her inability to communicate with Spanish-speaking students, she went to Guatemala in 1997 to learn their language.

Just before her return to the United States, Hanley visited Guatemala City and noticed entire families sifting through garbage at the municipal dump. These individuals, unschooled and beset by poverty, relied upon the dump for their livelihood. Hanley felt she could change the situation by sharing her talents as a teacher. In 1999, she instituted an educational program for the children of these families, calling it Camino Seguro, or Safe Passage. She also called upon others to share what they had, and who they were, with the children of the Guatemala City dump.

Traveling between Maine and Guatemala – and eventually to sites across the world – Hanley raised money and motivated an impressive number of Safe Passage volunteers. She also looked toward the future for the children who would be graduating from her program. Unfortunately, she was not to be a part of this future. On January 18, 2007, Hanley left the Safe Passage campus to visit a potential job-training site. Her car was hit by a bus traveling in the wrong direction. Hanley Denning was killed. She was 36 years old.

I learned of Hanley's death on January 19, 2007 – my 36th birthday. I had last seen her the previous spring at the Safe Passage 5K road race. We spoke briefly while waiting in line to use the bathroom, sharing a joke about the scarcity of women's facilities at races (all runners understand this inconvenient reality). Hanley had the same ready smile, the same goofy sense of humor. This time, however, she seemed tired. I resolved to do what I could to help my Bowdoin College classmate and high school friend.

I did not have a chance to fulfill this promise before Hanley died. But I have made an effort to do so since, and this effort has perhaps been even more meaningful than it otherwise would have been. In a strange twist, Hanley had told her parents that previous Christmas that she believed her life would soon be cut short. Concerned about the fate of Safe Passage, she asked her parents to ensure that "her children" would continue to be cared for, and that her mission would be continued. **our daily tread** represents my contribution to this mission — and the contributions of many, many others.

By purchasing **our daily tread** you, too, are contributing to Hanley's mission, as all proceeds will go directly to the children of Safe Passage.

Thank you for sharing what you have with others.
May you undertake your journey deliberately, and with joy.

Lisa M. Belisle, M.D., M.P.H.
October 2008

JOHN SANTERRE

MIKE GLAD

the story of Safe Passage

THE SCENE IS UNIMAGINABLE: Hundreds of families scavenge at the largest garbage dump in Central America amid toxic fumes and circling vultures. They are looking for anything to eat, recycle or resell. Of the nearly 3,000 people searching daily, most earn no more than $4 per day for their efforts. Children, mothers, fathers, and grandparents depend upon a deep ravine of trash for their survival.

Maine native Hanley Denning found herself a witness to this desperate situation. "There were flies everywhere, the smells were horrific…and I was struck by how many children, some of them hardly old enough to walk, were working in the garbage dump. It was amazing to learn that many of them had never been in school – that really the garbage dump was their only reality."

Knowing she could not turn away from this reality, Hanley created the educational organization Camino Seguro, also known as Safe Passage. In Guatemala, education is a "universal right," but for the poor who can't afford the minimum fees, textbooks and uniforms required to attend public schools, it is an impossible dream. Hanley's inspiration was to build upon the foundation of existing resources and meet the real needs and aspirations of the garbage dump community dwellers.

The beginnings of Safe Passage were humble. Hanley raised the first-year budget, a modest $5,000, by selling her belongings and writing a small grant proposal. This enabled a few dozen children to crowd into an abandoned cinder-block chapel for tutoring and a much-needed meal. Hanley's project blossomed as she inspired countless teachers, social workers, volunteers and financial supporters from around the world to join her efforts.

In the Safe Passage program, children attend public school (which in Guatemala is half-day) through the financial support of sponsors and donors. They then receive learning reinforcement at the Safe Passage center. Safe Passage also provides them with a meal (often their only meal of the day), medical care, athletic activities, music, art and family services. Children and families experience the dignity of self-sufficiency and earn monthly food support as a reward for school attendance.

The typical child who enters the program cannot read or write and is often severely malnourished. Yet only a small percentage of students drop out of Safe Passage's program and many students exceed the average academic performance of all Guatemalan students. In 2007, several Safe Passage students were enrolled in top Guatemalan private schools as a result of the students' exceptional academic merit.

The real achievement of Safe Passage can be read in the eyes of children who now have hope for the future, and in the determination of adolescents who now dream of life beyond the garbage dump. It can be understood in the persistence of mothers who attend Safe Passage's adult literacy programs and are learning to read and write. Even more fundamental than providing educational opportunities, Safe Passage gives the children and families of the garbage dump a reason to believe that they matter.

Following Hanley's tragic death in 2007, a committed group of people came together to ensure the ongoing success of her vision. Today, Safe Passage is led by director Barbara Nijhuis, a Dutch woman who is deeply dedicated to Guatemala and its people. Nearly 500 children fill the bright facilities at Safe Passage, including a new day-care center with play fields and gardens. These serve as places of peace and hope in a seemingly hopeless environment. In addition to changing the lives of Guatemalan children, Safe Passage has had a deep impact on people from Hanley's home state and around the world. Hundreds of individuals travel to Guatemala to volunteer each year, while numerous regional Safe Passage friends groups provide continued support to the program.

Paul Sutherland, the former chairman of Safe Passage's board of directors, likes to say that his fondest hope is that one day a graduate of Safe Passage will be elected president of Guatemala. Shortly after Hanley's death, Guatemala's then first lady Wendy Berger visited Safe Passage with United States first lady Laura Bush. At a meeting with the first ladies, a young Safe Passage student articulated his dream to be "El Presidente" some day. With a commitment to hard work, with continued leadership and support, and with Hanley's spirit in mind, the children, families and supporters of Safe Passage believe that anything is possible!

Tim Paradis, Jane Gallagher and the Safe Passage staff

JOHN SANTERRE

using **our daily tread**

One of Hanley's greatest assets as a teacher was her ability to see the potential in others and ask others to act on this potential.

our daily tread may help you recognize your own potential:

Notice the theme given at the beginning of each month.
Set aside time each day for a brief walk or other solitary outing.
Reflect briefly on the monthly theme and daily quote.
Keep a journal of your musings.
Be reminded of your own abilities.
Live deliberately, and with joy.
Share what you have, and who you are, with others.

For other ideas, visit www.dailytread.com.

~LB

january

reflection

MIKE RITTER

1

New Year's Day

*Tell me, what is it you plan to do
with your one wild and precious life?*

MARY OLIVER

2

Never be afraid to sit a while and think.

LORRAINE HANSBERRY

3

*Have a mind that is open to everything
and attached to nothing.*

DR. WAYNE W. DYER

4

Whatsoever things are true
Whatsoever things are honest,
Whatsoever things are just,
Whatsoever things are pure,
Whatsoever things are lovely —

Think on these things.

PHILIPPIANS 4:8

5

To think about oneself is terrifying.
But it is the only honest thing:

To think about myself as I am,
My ugly features, my beautiful features,
And wonder at them.
What other solid beginning can I have,
what to make progress from except myself?

MARY HASKELL

6

Epiphany

There are only two ways to live your life.
One is as though nothing is a miracle.
The other is as though everything is a miracle.

ALBERT EINSTEIN

7

*Solitude is a silent storm that breaks down
all our dead branches.*

*Yet it sends our living roots deeper
into the living heart of the living earth.*

KAHLIL GIBRAN

8

If you don't know where you're from, you'll have a hard time saying where you're going.

WENDELL BERRY

9

Speed is irrelevant
if you are traveling in the wrong direction.

GANDHI

JOSEPH DELCONZO

10

The further back you can look,
the further forward you are likely to see.

WINSTON CHURCHILL

11

*The life of every man is a diary in which he means
to write one story, and writes another;
and his humblest hour is when he compares the
volume as it is with what he vowed to make it.*

SIR JAMES MATTHEW BARRIE

12

It is good that you have questions.
Concentrate, look around you, the answer is there.

TULKU TSEWANG

13

*What makes people despair is that they try
to find a universal meaning to the whole of life,
and then end up by saying it is absurd,
illogical, empty of meaning.*

*There is not one big cosmic meaning for all,
there is only the meaning we each give to our life, an
individual meaning, an individual plot,
like an individual novel, a book for each person.*

ANAÏS NIN

Rachel Meyn, Safe Passage

From "Hanley the Teacher"

Because of Hanley, I moved in the dead of winter to Maine, where I knew no one, to open the Safe Passage office. I agreed under the condition that I'd do anything for the program, but I was too nervous to speak in public. "I don't think I can do it." I was set on that. She saw the crack in that statement – I didn't THINK I could do it. One month later at about 10 p.m., I received a phone call from Hanley. She exclaimed, "Oh, Rach, can you do a HUGE favor for me?! I need you to do two presentations back-to-back starting at 8 a.m." I hardly slept that night, yet as I drove to the school where I'd be speaking Hanley called me to give me words of encouragement and to be my personal cheerleader.

Just as Hanley had given me the strength to do something that I thought was impossible, she gave strength to each and every child every day. She gave hope to volunteers and individuals around the world, who saw by her example that one person is absolutely capable of making a difference.

JOSEPH DELCONZO

14

Be patient toward all that is unsolved in your heart
and try to love the questions themselves,
like locked rooms and like books
that are written in a very foreign tongue.

Do not seek the answers, which cannot be given you
because you would not be able to live them. And the point is
to live everything. Live the questions now.
Perhaps you will then gradually, without noticing it,
live along some distant day into the answers.

RAINER MARIA RILKE

15

*The wars between peoples are a reflection
of our own inner conflict and fear.*

JACK KORNFIELD

16

He who conceals his disease cannot be cured.

ETHIOPIAN PROVERB

17

Most people are searching for happiness.
They're looking for it.
They're trying to find it in someone
or something outside of themselves.
That's a fundamental mistake.
Happiness is something that you are,
and it comes from the way you think.

Dr. Wayne W. Dyer

18

The storyteller makes no choice;
Soon you will not hear his voice.
His job is to shed light
And not to master.

ROBERT HUNTER

19

No man can reveal to you aught but that which already lies half asleep in the dawning of your knowledge. The teacher who walks in the shadow of the temple, among his followers, gives not of his wisdom but rather of his faith and his lovingness. If he is indeed wise, he does not bid you enter the house of his wisdom, but rather leads you to the threshold of your own mind.

KAHLIL GIBRAN

MIKE RITTER

20

Inauguration Day (United States)

Most powerful is he who has himself in his power.

LUCIUS ANNAEUS SENECA

21

The purpose of learning is growth, and our minds, unlike our bodies, can continue growing as we continue to live.

MORTIMER ADLER

22

Learning is wealth that can't be stolen.

PHILIPPINE PROVERB

23

Upon the subject of education...
I can only say that I view it
as the most important subject which we,
as a people,
may be engaged in.

ABRAHAM LINCOLN

JOSEPH DELCONZO

24

*We are now at a point where we must educate people
in what nobody knew yesterday, and
prepare in our schools for what no one knows yet
but what people must know tomorrow.*

Margaret Mead

25

*The whole purpose of education is
to turn mirrors into windows.*

SYDNEY J. HARRIS

26

No matter where you go or what you do, you live your entire life within the confines of your head.

TERRY JOSEPHSON

27

It is our mind, and that alone, that chains us or sets us free.

DILGO KHYENTSE RINPOCHE

28

We are what we think. All that arises with our thoughts. With our thoughts we make the world.

Buddha

29

We must be willing to get rid of the life we've planned, so as to have the life that is waiting for us.

Joseph Campbell

30

*Faith is an oasis in the heart
that will never be reached
by a caravan of thinking.*

KAHLIL GIBRAN

JOHN SANTERRE

31

*Intuition will tell the thinking mind
where to look next.*

DR. JONAS SALK

love and compassion

february

1

No one is born hating another person
because of the colour of his skin, or his
background or his religion. People must learn
to hate and, if they can learn to hate, they can be
taught to love, for love comes more naturally
to the human heart than its opposite.

NELSON MANDELA

2

Groundhog Day

*The individual is capable of both
great compassion and great indifference.
He has it within his means to nourish
the former and outgrow the latter.*

NORMAN COUSINS

JOHN SANTERRE

3

Love is discovered through the practice of loving, not by the words.

PAULO COELHO

4

For if I am to love truly and freely, I must be able to give something that is truly mine to another.

If my heart does not at first belong to me, how can I give it to another?

It is not mine to give.

THOMAS MERTON

5

Time is too slow for those who wait,
too swift for those who fear,
too long for those who grieve,
too short for those who rejoice,
but for those who love,
time is eternity.

HENRY VAN DYKE

6

The heart has its reasons which reason knows not of.

BLAISE PASCAL

7

*To love at all is like trying to remember
the tune and words to a song that the spirits
have given you in your sleep.*

LOUISE ERDRICH

8

Throw your heart over the fence
and the rest will follow.

NORMAN VINCENT PEALE

MIKE RITTER

9

*Love, compassion, joy and equanimity are the very nature of an enlightened person.
They are the four aspects of true love within ourselves and within everyone and everything.*

THICH NHAT HANH

10

Love hinders death. Love is life.
All, everything that I understand,
I understand only because I love.

Everything is, everything exists, only because
I love. Everything is united by it alone.
God is love.

LEO TOLSTOY

11

Compassion for ourselves gives rise to the power to transform resentment into forgiveness, hatred into friendliness, and fear into respect for all beings.

JACK KORNFIELD

12

Abraham Lincoln's Birthday

To thine own self be true,
And it must follow, as the night the day,
Thou canst not then be false to any man.

WILLIAM SHAKESPEARE

13

*I've learned that some people will forget
what you said, people will forget what you did,
but people will never forget
how you made them feel.*

Maya Angelou

14

Valentine's Day

Thee lift me, and I'll lift thee,
and we'll ascend together.

QUAKER PROVERB

15

Love consists in this: That two solitudes protect and touch and greet each other.

RAINER MARIA RILKE

16

To get the full value of a joy, you must have somebody to divide it with.

MARK TWAIN

17

The most I can do for my friend is simply to be
his friend. I have no wealth to bestow on him.
If he knows I am happy in loving him,
he will want no other reward.
Is not friendship divine in this?

HENRY DAVID THOREAU

ANTONIA MUNROE

18

Friendship marks a life even more deeply than love.

ELIE WIESEL

19

There's a kind of emotional exploration
you plumb with a friend
that you don't really do with your family.

BETTE MIDLER

20

Friendship is the comfort,
the inexpressible comfort of
feeling safe with a person —
having neither to weigh thoughts
nor measure words.

GEORGE ELIOT

21

*No pessimist ever discovered
the secrets of the stars,
or sailed to an uncharted land,
or opened a heart to the human spirit.*

Helen Keller

22

George Washington's Birthday

One can live magnificently in the world if one knows how to work and how to love.

LEO TOLSTOY

23

Let the beauty you love be what you do.
There are a thousand ways to kneel and kiss the earth.

RUMI

Monique Jamine, long-term Safe Passage volunteer, the Netherlands

From "Like Honey to Bees"

What was it about Hanley that made her so attractive and charismatic? I think it was her sincere love and genuine care for children — all children. That love and care was so strong that it was not only felt by children, but by everyone who met her... The image comes to my mind of her swimming in Lago de Atitlán — a gorgeous lake in Guatemala where I spent my last days as a long-term volunteer of Safe Passage. As she is swimming, she is in no time surrounded by three indigenous kids who don't know her. Truly, she never met these kids before, but they are drawn to her, playing and having fun with her — not with any of the other adults, just with Hanley. As I see that image of her and these children in the lake, I think of the attraction kids felt for her: "Like Honey to Bees."

Hanley was relentlessly giving of herself. There was no postponing or waiting of any kind when it came to improving the situation of the children. Maybe that was at the heart of her beauty and where she got her energy from, that relentless and disciplined giving to others. Isn't that exactly what makes any one of us beautiful and alive?

JOSEPH DELCONZO

MIKE RITTER

24

You do not have to be good.
You do not have to walk on your knees
For a hundred miles through the desert repenting.
You only have to let the soft animal of your body
Love what it loves.

MARY OLIVER

25

The true way to soften one's troubles is to solace those of others.

<small>MADAME DE MAINTENON</small>

26

*It doesn't interest me if there is one God
or many gods. I want to know if you know
how to fall into that fierce heat of living.
I want to know if you are willing to live
day by day with the consequence of love.*

DAVID WHYTE

27

Think not that you can direct the course of love.
For love, if it finds you worthy, directs your course.

KAHLIL GIBRAN

JOHN SANTERRE

28

Whenever you are confronted with an opponent,
conquer him with love.

GANDHI

29

Few of us can do great things, but all of us
can do small things with great love.

MOTHER TERESA

hope

march

1

*How lovely to think that nobody
need wait a single moment
before beginning to improve the world.*

ANNE FRANK

2

The very least you can do in your life
is to figure out what you hope for.
And the most you can do is live inside that hope.
Not admire it from a distance,
but live right in it, under its roof.

BARBARA KINGSOLVER

3

Just as despair can come to one only from other human beings, hope, too, can be given to one only by other human beings.

ELIE WIESEL

4

There is no time for destruction, hate or anger. We must build on hope.

LEO TOLSTOY

5

Often, I too am overcome by the hatred, the jealousy and envy,
the wars, all the ugliness that is part of our world.
I try to live in beauty and goodness; I seek out all that has
a quality of inner beauty, and I am immediately repulsed
by anything ugly that sends out bad vibrations.
Over the years, I have tried very hard to create and build up
within me a kind of beauty and spiritual strength,
so that I always have this to turn to when the harshness
of the world becomes too depressing.

RAVI SHANKAR

6

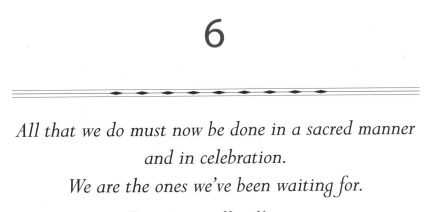

All that we do must now be done in a sacred manner
and in celebration.
We are the ones we've been waiting for.

Elders of the Hopi Nation

7

*The difference between what we do
and what we are capable of doing would suffice
to solve most of the world's problems.*

GANDHI

8

The future depends entirely
on what each of us does every day.
A movement is only people moving.

GLORIA STEINEM

Marina Denning, Hanley's mother

When Hanley was home the Christmas before she died, she asked me what I thought the purpose of life was. I told her that I felt that "the purpose of life is a life of purpose." I remember thinking that perhaps that answer was too simplistic. After Hanley's death, I elaborated on my answer to Hanley's Christmas question in the form of a poem. I shared this on March 9, 2007, with those who had gathered for the first Maine showing of "Recycled Lives" – a documentary about the children of the Guatemalan dumps. This was offered as a gift to her on what would have been her 37th birthday.

Happy birthday, my beloved Hanley, with infinite love.

Hanley's Answer

*A life which passes on and leaves no mark is for the man
to whom there is no singing bird — no golden passageway.*

*To him who knows no dawn with opal banners
flung around a dream, there is no hope.*

*Years are as lives; when each is richly full of sweet love,
symphony and chime of children's laughter.*

*Only to him who truly loves can come the peace and joy
of hands outstretched against the night.*

MARINA DENNING

JOSEPH DELCONZO

9

Hanley's Birthday

*I believe that the rendering of useful service
is the common duty of mankind and that only
in the purifying fire of sacrifice is the dross
of selfishness consumed and the greatness
of the human soul set free.*

JOHN D. ROCKEFELLER JR.

10

If your life is broken and poured out,
it can feed a multitude versus a whole loaf
that may only feed one small boy.

ELISABETH ELLIOT

11

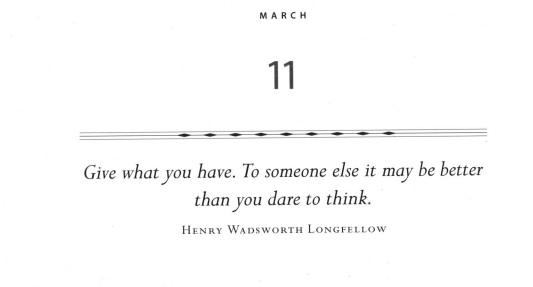

*Give what you have. To someone else it may be better
than you dare to think.*

HENRY WADSWORTH LONGFELLOW

ANTONIA MUNROE

12

If you hold your hand closed, nothing good can come in. The open hand is blessed, for it gives in abundance, even as it receives.

BIDDY MASON

13

*Instead of wondering whether or not
we can save the planet, it is best to ignore such
trivialities and simply get to work.*

FRITJOF CAPRA

14

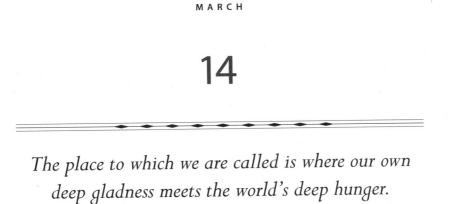

The place to which we are called is where our own deep gladness meets the world's deep hunger.

FREDERICK BUECHNER

15

If I can stop one Heart from breaking
I shall not live in vain
If I can ease one Life the Aching,
Or cool one Pain

Or help one fainting Robin
Unto his Nest again
I shall not live in vain.

EMILY DICKINSON

16

*Sometimes when I consider what tremendous
consequences come from little things…
I am tempted to think…
there are no little things.*

BRUCE BARTON

17

St. Patrick's Day

*St. Patrick's Day is an enchanted time —
a day to begin transforming winter's dreams
into summer's magic.*

ADRIENNE COOK

18

*True heroism is remarkably sober,
very undramatic. It is not the urge
to surpass all others at whatever
cost, but the urge to serve others
at whatever cost.*

Arthur Ashe

93

Jordan Denning, Hanley's brother

I have pictures, some unbeknownst to my mother, of my sister and me at three, four, and five years old. She was older and quite a bit taller for some time. In each picture she is holding my hand, or has an arm around me, or is running on the beach while I toddle behind her. As adults, she took on much the same role. With every one of life's ups and downs, whether it was professional or personal, Han was there to provide her best guidance to me, her little brother.

In our rather raucous household of two, then three, brothers, Hanley maintained a commitment to excellence in all she did. Seth, Lucas and I were more likely to be found wrestling in our yard or playing Nerf ball in the house (much to our mother's chagrin) than pulling all-nighters to ensure we aced an exam. So we did not always know what to make of our sister's truly remarkable dedication to her goals — especially when she was a teenager. Barricaded in her bedroom and surrounded by books and posters of her idols, from Joan Benoit Samuelson to Gandhi, we often worried that Hanley worked too hard, that she was so intensely focused on doing it the right way that she was missing out on what we considered "fun."

We later realized that our sister was a unique individual. We learned that the personal courage it took never to quit on her dreams and to follow through until results were in hand would enable Hanley to create Safe Passage from nothing and against seemingly insurmountable odds.

PHIL KIRCHNER

Lucas Denning and Safe Passage friends

Today, my brothers and I are still able to draw on our big sister's example. I must admit that when the chips are down, I will whisper to Han and ask what she might do in a given situation. And I will report on the latest news: "Han, you'd be so proud of Lucas." Or, "Han, you should see how big Sethie's kids are getting." Then I listen very, very closely, and I'll be damned if I don't hear in a nearly inaudible tone…

"I know, Jord. I know. Be happy."

19

During dry periods an ant colony, like those of all social insects, is in mortal danger of desiccation. In my view, the sharing of food and water is a more important component of advanced social behavior than dominance, leadership, or another kind of interaction.

E.O. WILSON

20

The main thing is to care. Care very hard, even if it is only a game you are playing.

BILLIE JEAN KING

21

Guard well within yourself that treasure, kindness. Know how to give without hesitation, how to lose without regret, how to acquire without meanness.

GEORGE SAND

22

If I could only speak one prayer for you, my children,
it would be that your hearts would not only beat
but grow ever greater in gratitude.

KATE BRAESTRUP

23

Do not ask yourself what the world needs.
Ask yourself what makes you come alive
and go do that, because what the world needs
is people who come alive.

GIL BAILIE

MIKE RITTER

24

The power of a movement lies in the fact that it can indeed change the habits of people.

STEPHEN BANTU BIKO

25

You whose day it is
Make it beautiful
Get out your rainbow colors
So it will be beautiful.

NOOTKA, NORTH AMERICAN INDIAN TRIBE

26

Never doubt that a small group of thoughtful people
could change the world.
Indeed, it's the only thing that ever has.

MARGARET MEAD

27

The life I touch for good or ill
will touch another life, and that in turn another,
until who knows where the trembling stops
or in what far place my touch will be felt.

FREDERICK BUECHNER

28

We can't do everything for everyone everywhere, but we can do something for someone somewhere.

RICHARD L. EVANS

JOHN SANTERRE

MIKE RITTER

Chip Griffin, volunteer and sponsor

From "Vacation with a Mission"

We first traveled to Guatemala in 2004 to enjoy the eternal spring and ancient ruins. While there, we also ventured out to view the incredible poverty of the vast Guatemala City garbage dump. It reminded us of Ground Zero just after 9/11. Since then, my family and I have returned several times to volunteer with Safe Passage. On one such trip, I met the child my family sponsors, four-year-old Marco Tulio. We hugged each other and tossed a Frisbee on the lawn at the main building of Safe Passage, where Hanley Denning watched us from her office.

Hanley knew Marco Tulio, as she personally understood each and every one of the 500 impoverished dump children in her program. She and I had visited Marco Tulio's home, about 10 feet by 12 feet of makeshift materials with a dirt floor of reclaimed dump land where the methane fumes seep up through the ground. No power, no lights, no bathroom, no stove or fridge, no running water, and no windows or doors.

Only one mattress was cast in the corner, where Marco Tulio's mom told me that seven of their family members lived and slept in this tiny, grimy, and dark space...

29

Never do things others can do and will do
if there are things others cannot do and will not do.

AMELIA EARHART

30

I know of no more encouraging fact than the unquestionable
ability of man to elevate his life by a conscious endeavor.
It is something to be able to paint a particular image, or to carve
a statue, and so to make a few objects beautiful; but it is far more
glorious to carve and paint the very atmosphere and medium
through which we look, which morally we can do.
To affect the quality of the day, that is the highest art.

HENRY DAVID THOREAU

31

At first, people refuse to believe that a strange new thing can be done, and then they begin to hope it can be done. Then they see it can be done — then it is done and all the world wonders why it was not done centuries ago.

FRANCES HODGSON BURNETT

mindfulness

april

1

*A wise man ought to realize that health
is his most valuable possession.*

HIPPOCRATES

MIKE RITTER

2

No one can listen to your body for you.
To grow and heal, you have to take responsibility
for listening to yourself.

JON KABAT-ZINN

3

Two roads diverged in a wood, and I —
I took the one less traveled by,
And that has made all the difference.

ROBERT FROST

MIKE RITTER

4

The press of my foot to the earth springs
a hundred affections.

WALT WHITMAN

5

There is something infinitely healing in the repeated
refrains of nature — the assurance
that dawn comes after night, and spring
after the winter.

RACHEL CARSON

6

I only went out for a walk
and finally concluded to stay out till sundown,
for going out, I found, was really going in.

JOHN MUIR

7

The greatest wealth is health.

VIRGIL

8

A faithful friend is the medicine of life.

APOCRYPHA

9

When we try to pick out anything by itself,
we find it hitched to everything else in the universe.

JOHN MUIR

10

*All big things in this world
are done by people who are naïve and have
an idea that is obviously impossible.*

FRANK RICHARDS

11

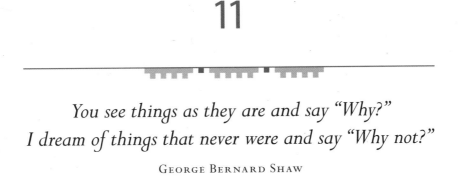

You see things as they are and say "Why?"
I dream of things that never were and say "Why not?"

GEORGE BERNARD SHAW

12

Be open to your dreams, people.
Embrace that distant shore
Because our mortal journey
Is over all too soon.

David Assael

13

Sometimes we end up doing what we are capable of whether we like it or not.

ANNA QUINDLEN

14

Thomas Jefferson's Birthday

*We cannot do everything, and there is
a sense of liberation in realizing that.
This enables us to do something, and to
do it very well. It may be incomplete,
but it is a beginning, a step along the way.*

OSCAR ROMERO

15

Dream as if you'll live forever, live as if you'll die today.

James Dean

JOHN SANTERRE

Jon Torres, Safe Passage volunteer

From "Hello, Doctor"
(Adapted from the *Lewiston Sun Journal*, May 6, 2007)

I found I was naïve in thinking I could give the bottle of amoxicillin I brought with me to a sick child: The family had no way to keep the medicine refrigerated. I was naïve in failing to ask a 10-year-old Guatemalan boy about his line of work when he appeared with back pain. It didn't occur to me that the boy was carrying heavy material on his back and strapped to his head on weekends. I was saddened to learn many local people, including children, sniff glue and solvents to escape their environment, at least for a while. I saw how quickly things expanded from a one-on-one encounter to a public health concern — a huge concern — but only one of many for this area and these people.

16

If one advances confidently in the direction of his dreams and endeavors to live the life which he has imagined, he will meet with a success unexpected in common hours.

HENRY DAVID THOREAU

17

Hold fast to dreams for if dreams die,
life is a broken-winged bird that cannot fly.

LANGSTON HUGHES

18

Daily duties and daily bread
Are the sweetest things in life.

ROBERT LOUIS STEVENSON

19

As soon as you trust yourself,
you will know how to live.

JOHANN WOLFGANG VON GOETHE

MIKE RITTER

How swiftly the strained honey
Of afternoon light
Flows into darkness

And the closed bud shrugs off
Its special mystery
In order to break into blossom

As if what exists, exists
So that it can be lost
And become precious.

LISEL MUELLER

21

All serious daring starts from within.

EUDORA WELTY

22

*According to Buddhism, the life of all beings —
human, animal, or otherwise — is precious, and all have
the same right to happiness. It is certain that birds, wild
animals — all the creatures inhabiting our planet — are
our companions. They are a part of our world;
we share it with them.*

THE 14TH DALAI LAMA

23

What lies behind us and what lies before us are small matters compared to what lies within us.

RALPH WALDO EMERSON

24

Perfect health, like perfect beauty, is a rare thing; and so, it seems, is perfect disease.

PETER MERE LATHAM

25

*It is very strange that when you set a goal for yourself,
it is hard not to hold toward it
even if it is inconvenient or not even desirable.*

JOHN STEINBECK

26

Learn to be quiet enough to hear the genuine within yourself, so that you can hear it in others.

MARIAN WRIGHT EDELMAN

27

*Something in me wanted to find out how far
I could run without stopping.*

JACKI HANSON

MIKE RITTER

28

The human body can only do so much.
Then the heart and spirit must take over.

SOHN KEE-CHUNG

29

Every great dream begins with a dreamer.
Always remember, you have within you the strength,
the patience, and the passion to reach for the stars
to change the world.

HARRIET TUBMAN

30

You must do the thing you think you cannot do!

Eleanor Roosevelt

courage

may

1

Whatever you can do, or dream you can, begin it.
Boldness has genius, power and magic in it.

JOHANN WOLFGANG VON GOETHE

2

Do not go where your path may lead, go instead where there is no path and leave a trail.

RALPH WALDO EMERSON

3

*There came a time when the risk to remain
tight in the bud was more painful than the risk
it took to blossom.*

ANAÏS NIN

4

Living is a form of not being sure, not knowing what's next or how. We guess. We may be wrong, but we take leap after leap in the dark.

AGNES DE MILLE

JOSEPH DELCONZO

5

Don't let life discourage you; everyone who got where he is had to be where he was.

RICHARD L. EVANS

6

If you don't live it, it won't come out of your horn.

CHARLIE PARKER

7

It takes courage to grow up and turn out to be who you really are.

E.E. CUMMINGS

8

*Courage is not the absence of fear
but rather the judgment that something else
is more important than fear.*

AMBROSE REDMOON

9

Only those who risk going too far can possibly find out how far they can go.

T.S. ELIOT

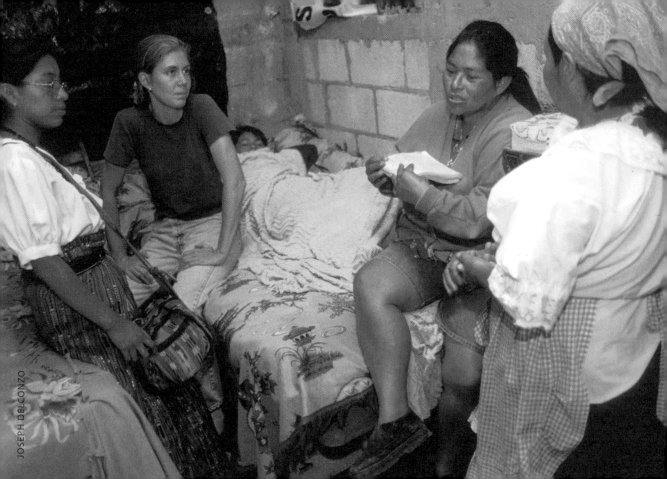

JOSEPH DELCONZO

10

Courage is what it takes to stand up and speak;
it is also what it takes to sit down and listen.

WINSTON CHURCHILL

11

Our deepest fear is not that we are inadequate.
Our deepest fear is that we are powerful beyond measure.
We ask ourselves, who am I to be brilliant, gorgeous, talented,
fabulous? Actually, who are you not to be? We were born
to make manifest the glory of God that is within us.
As we let our own light shine, we unconsciously
give others permission to do the same.

MARIANNE WILLIAMSON

JOSEPH DELCONZO

12

*Life shrinks or expands
in proportion
to one's courage.*

ANAÏS NIN

13

The way you overcome shyness is to become so wrapped up in something you forget to be afraid.

LADY BIRD JOHNSON

14

We can throw stones, complain about them, stumble on them, climb over them, or build with them.

WILLIAM ARTHUR WARD

15

Explanations don't explain. Excuses don't excuse.
They just build bridges to nowhere
and monuments to nothing.

ANONYMOUS

16

*Noise proves nothing — often a hen
who has merely laid an egg cackles
as if she had laid an asteroid.*

MARK TWAIN

17

*All the beautiful sentiments
in the world weigh less than
a single lovely action.*

James Russell Lowell

18

Practice what you know, and it will help make clear what now you do not know.

REMBRANDT

19

We are what we repeatedly do.
Excellence then is not an act, but a habit.

ARISTOTLE

JOSEPH DELCONZO

20

Do not mistake "talk" for "action."
Pity fills no stomach.
Compassion builds no houses.

SHIMON BEN GAMLIEL

21

The guy who takes a chance, who walks the line between the known and unknown, who is unafraid of failure, will succeed.

GORDON PARKS

22

*We have no choice of what color we're born or who
our parents are or whether we're rich or poor.
What we do have is some choice over what we make
of our lives once we're here.*

MILDRED D. TAYLOR

JOSEPH DELCONZO

23

*You gain strength, courage and confidence
by every experience in which you really stop
to look fear in the face.*

ELEANOR ROOSEVELT

Jane Gallagher, Safe Passage volunteer, child sponsor

I was hoping against hope that I would not get assigned to the lice shampoo station. I'd been hugging and playing with kids all week long and had enjoyed the contact and the closeness, but for some reason, thinking about that lice station caused me great anxiety. Of course, when assignments were given out, not only was I assigned to combing head lice, I was put in charge of it! I resigned myself to the task. It wouldn't be that bad. I could deal with this. All morning I worked on combing head lice from the hair of these beautiful children who literally lived down in the dumps. At lunch I was so tired I wanted to curl up in a corner and go to sleep. After lunch I paced myself, knowing that in a few hours, I would be on a plane heading to comfort and cleanliness and peace – leaving this place of grime, garbage, smells and sights so sad I couldn't process them all at once. Every time I heard a plane overhead I welled up with tears, thinking that I can go home, but these kids, my sponsored kids and the ones I'd come to love during that week, would be still here tomorrow and tomorrow and tomorrow.

At last it was time to clean up and leave. It was about 4:15, and we were supposed to pack up our station at 4:00. A young girl came over and asked for a lice shampoo and combing. Every shred of my being wanted to say, "sorry, it's too late," but for some reason, all of us who were still working at that station smiled and said, "It's OK, come on over." I was done, cooked, spent, hollowed out at that point and seriously questioned whether or not I could do it. I felt so frail and vulnerable. As I looked at this beautiful young girl, I knew that I could do this: I could comb her long, tangled, lice-riddled hair. I could do it by starting very small and working my way through one bit at a time. Another volunteer from Maine was working with me, and as we began to untangle the little girl's hair, I began to feel something inside me untangle, too. With each stroke, I felt a bit more relaxed and a bit less empty, a bit more filled up. What was filling me up was love. As I cared for this child, this stranger to me a few minutes before, I was getting back this amazing, overwhelming sense of peace. I knew that few things I'd done in my life were as important as what I was doing at that moment.

24

Walk with the dreamers, the believers, the courageous, the cheerful, the planners, the doers. The successful people with their heads in the clouds and their feet on the ground. Let their spirit ignite a fire within you to leave this world better than when you found it.

WILFRED PETERSEN

25

One day you finally knew
What you had to do, and began.

MARY OLIVER

26

There is an inmost center in us all where
truth abides in fullness
and to know rather consists in opening out a way
where the imprisoned splendor may escape
than in effecting entrance for a light supposed
to be without.

ROBERT BROWNING

27

The bitterest tears shed over graves are for words left unsaid and deeds left undone.

HARRIET BEECHER STOWE

28

Be glad today. Tomorrow may bring tears.
Be brave today. The darkest night will pass.
And golden rays will usher in the dawn.

SARAH KNOWLES BOLTON

29

We are not living in eternity.
We have only this moment, sparking like a star
in our hand and melting like a snowflake.

MARIE BEYNON RAY

30

Memorial Day

*If you would hit the mark, you must aim
a little above it. Every arrow that flies
feels the attraction of earth.*

HENRY WADSWORTH LONGFELLOW

MIKE RITTER

31

I'm not old enough to play baseball or football.
I'm not eight yet. My mom told me,
when you start baseball, you aren't going to
be able to run that fast because you had an
operation. I told mom I wouldn't need to run that fast.
When I play baseball, I'll just hit them out of the park.
Then I'll be able to walk.

EDWARD J. MCGRATH

perseverance

june

1

Worrying does not empty tomorrow of its troubles,
it empties today of its strength.

MARY ENGELBREIT

2

*The ultimate measure of a man
is not where he stands in moments of comfort
and convenience, but where he stands
at times of challenge and controversy.*

Martin Luther King Jr.

3

It's possible, even in the midst of hardship,
to experience simple pleasures. To know delight,
what's right and beautiful in the world.
With mental balance, we develop a keel-like ballast
that helps us to remain stable
even under extreme conditions.

JON KABAT-ZINN

4

*Perseverance is a great element of success.
If you only knock long enough at the gate,
you are sure to wake up somebody.*

HENRY WADSWORTH LONGFELLOW

5

Achievements start when you know that your present place in life does not determine how far you will go. Its only purpose is to remind you where you started.

KEITH HARRELL

6

The strongest force in the world is gentleness.

HAN SUYIN

7

Energy and persistence conquer all things.

BENJAMIN FRANKLIN

JOHN SANTERRE

8

Tomorrow is fresh with no mistakes in it.

Lucy Maud Montgomery

9

Write the wrongs that are done to you in the sand,
but write the good things that happen to you
on a piece of marble. Let go of all emotions such
as resentment and retaliation, which diminish you,
and hold onto the emotions, such as gratitude
and joy, which increase you.

ARABIC SAYING

10

Toldos Yaakov Yosef offers an allegorical rendering. In order to ascend a mountain, one must free himself of excess baggage and bulky clothing so that he may travel as lightly as possible. This is doubly true in the attempt to scale spiritual heights. One who is unencumbered by the weight of possessions and social commitments can be light in order to rise to the top.

PIRKEI AVOS: ETHICS OF OUR FATHERS

11

Let the world know you as you are,
not as you think you should be,
because sooner or later, if you are posing, you will
forget the pose, and then where are you?

FANNY BRICE

MIKE RITTER

12

Be bold, and mighty forces will come to your aid.

BASIL KING

13

Finish each day and be done with it.
You have done what you could.
Some blunders and absurdities have crept in;
Forget them as soon as you can.
Tomorrow is a new day.
You shall begin it serenely and with too high a spirit
To be encumbered with your old nonsense.

RALPH WALDO EMERSON

14

Flag Day

*Any intelligent fool can make things bigger, more
complex and more violent. It takes a touch
of genius — and a lot of courage — to move
in the opposite direction.*

ALBERT EINSTEIN

15

The lure of the distant and difficult is deceptive.
The great opportunity is where you are.

JOHN BURROUGHS

16

A journey of a thousand miles
begins with a single step.

LAO TSE

17

Winners forget they are in a race;
they just love to run.

WILLIAM MASTROSIMONE

18

A new philosophy, a new way of life, is not given for nothing. It has to be paid for and only acquired with much patience and great effort.

FYODOR DOSTOEVSKY

MIKE GLAD

Paul Sutherland, Safe Passage board member

From "Excellence is Not Competitive"

"Who do we throw out? Paul? Who? Come on, which kid?" Tears dripped down her freckled, flushed face. I had watched red grow up Hanley's neck like an old-fashioned thermometer's mercury rising to the top. I had seen Hanley's rage before — we were friends. I was her mentor and confidant, so I had learned to let her boil over because we had agreed she could show her frustration, fears and weariness to me, for that was our communication/friendship agreement: Everything goes. We could ask anything of each other, and she could ask anything of me in confidence. So here we were in a conference room a thousand miles from Guatemala. Someone had lobbed out the idea as an option to remedy our struggling finances that we reduce the number of children. That had caused Hanley to call a break, as she gave me the "follow me" look.

As I listened to Hanley state her case for keeping every child but limiting new children until financial support was there for them, I assessed this passionate woman. What was inside Hanley that allowed her to be such an effective leader? She was about excellence. Not the excellence that says, "I am better than someone else." Hanley's type of excellence said, "I take responsibility to act right in this situation and to do my best." In front of me stood Hanley: red-faced, tears in her eyes, sleep-deprived, weary and challenged by a suggestion that threatened her children. Before me stood a woman calling up the adrenaline from somewhere deep inside to act heroically one more time to help her children.

19

Work is and always has been my salvation,
and I thank the Lord for it.

LOUISA MAY ALCOTT

20

What is to give light must endure burning.

VIKTOR FRANKL

21

The breeze at dawn has secrets to tell you.
Don't go back to sleep.
You must ask for what you really want.
Don't go back to sleep.
People are going back and forth
Across the doorsill
Where the two worlds touch.
The door is round and open.
Don't go back to sleep.

RUMI

22

Those who contemplate the beauty of the earth find reserves of strength that will endure as long as life lasts.

RACHEL CARSON

23

God didn't promise days without pain,
laughter without sorrow,
sun without rain.
But He did promise strength for the day,
Comfort for tears, and light for the way.

ANONYMOUS

24

Our patience will achieve more than our force.

Edmund Burke

25

He who has a why can endure any how.

FRIEDRICH NIETZSCHE

DANIELLE TORRES

26

Success comes in cans;
failures come in can'ts.

ANONYMOUS

27

*Man will occasionally stumble over the truth
but usually manages to pick himself up,
walk over or around it, and carry on.*

WINSTON CHURCHILL

28

I know God won't give me anything I can't handle.
I just wish He didn't trust me so much.

MOTHER TERESA

29

At any moment the fully present mind can shatter
time and burst into Now.

DAVID STEINDL-RAST

30

Every success begins with two words:
I'll try.

ABBY BELISLE HALEY

growth

july

1

We are here, charged with the task of completing (one might say creating) ourselves.

WILLIAM COOK

2

✕◇✕

We write our own destiny; we become what we do.

MADAME CHIANG KAI-SHEK

3

You can't separate peace from freedom because no one can be at peace unless he has his freedom.

MALCOLM X

ANTONIA MUNROE

4

Independence Day

⬦⬦⬦⬦⬦⬦⬦⬦⬦⬦⬦⬦⬦⬦⬦⬦⬦⬦⬦⬦⬦⬦⬦⬦⬦⬦⬦⬦⬦⬦⬦⬦⬦⬦⬦

*A man who takes away another man's freedom
is a prisoner of hatred, he is locked behind the bars of prejudice
and narrow-mindedness. I am not truly free if I am
taking away someone else's freedom just as surely
as I am not free when my freedom is taken from me.
The oppressed and the oppressor alike
are robbed of their humanity.*

NELSON MANDELA

5

Freedom is something that dies unless it is used.

HUNTER S. THOMPSON

6

Does the road wind uphill all the way?
Yes, to the very end. Will the day's journey take the whole
long day? From morn to night, my friend.

CHRISTINA ROSSETTI

7

<>◇◇<

People often say that motivation doesn't last.
Well, neither does bathing —
that's why we recommend it daily.

ZIG ZIGLAR

MIKE RITTER

8

*Go forth on your path, as it exists
only through your walking.*

St. Augustine

9

Motivation is a battle for the heart,
not just an appeal to the mind.
Passion is always an expression of the soul.

PATRICK DIXON

10

Wheresoever you go,
Go with all your heart.

CONFUCIUS

◇◇

11

I carry your heart.
I carry it in my heart.

E.E. CUMMINGS

Beth Kloser, long-term Safe Passage volunteer

The donated vacant plot was a barren wasteland. Formerly part of the Guatemala City garbage dump, hard-packed dirt covered layers of unseen trash. Vultures circled overhead. The area was grim and colorless, matching its surroundings.

To Hanley Denning it was a virtual "field of dreams." She enthusiastically envisioned a park. It would have plants and green grass — a rare commodity in Zone 3 of Guatemala City. Most importantly, it held the potential to be a cheery, safe place for children to play and families to congregate. At that time, it was unknown when this vision would bear fruit, due to funding constraints.

In 2006, Hanley's "field of dreams" was turned into reality. Finally, there were inviting benches, colorful plants, flowers, and yes, green grass on which to play. At the dedication many adults tried to put into words the impact this green space would have on the local community. They spoke words of eloquence and hope. For me, however, the most powerful witness came from a little boy sitting next to me. As the adults continued to speak, he pointed and excitedly whispered, "Mire!" *Look!* My gaze followed his finger. In a thrilled voice, he said "una mariposa!" In this oasis from the grim realities of the garbage dump, a lovely butterfly hovered over a newly planted flower...

12

✶✶✶✶✶✶✶✶✶✶✶✶✶✶✶✶✶✶✶✶✶✶✶✶✶✶✶✶✶✶✶✶✶✶✶✶✶✶✶

The real voyage of discovery
Consists not in seeking new landscapes
But in having new eyes.

MARCEL PROUST

13

✥✥✥✥✥✥✥✥✥✥✥✥✥✥✥✥✥✥✥✥✥✥✥✥✥✥✥✥✥✥✥✥✥

Anything we fully do is an alone journey.

Natalie Goldberg

14

Discovery consists of looking at the same thing as everyone else and thinking something different.

ROGER VON OECH

ANTONIA MUNROE

15

×◇×

*Loneliness is and always has been the central
and inevitable experience of every man.*

THOMAS WOLFE

16

✕✕✕

Stand before the people you fear and speak your mind,
even if your voice shakes.

MAGGIE KUHN

17

*You have to leave the city of your comfort
and go into the wilderness of your intuition.
What you will discover will be wonderful.
What you will discover will be yourself.*

ALAN ALDA

18

✕◇✕

Our real journey in life is interior,
a matter of growth, deepening and an ever
greater surrender to the creative action of love
and grace in our hearts.

THOMAS MERTON

JOHN SANTERRE

19

You will either step forward into growth,
or you will step back into safety.

ABRAHAM MASLOW

✕◇✕◇✕◇✕◇✕◇✕◇✕◇✕◇✕◇✕◇✕◇✕◇✕◇✕◇✕◇✕◇✕◇✕◇✕◇✕

20

The essential conditions of everything you do must
be choice, love, passion.

NADIA BOULANGER

21

Be not afraid of growing slowly;
Be afraid only of standing still.

CHINESE PROVERB

22

To know the road ahead, ask those coming back.

CHINESE PROVERB

23

You cannot stay on the summit forever; you have to come down again...
So, why bother in the first place? Just this: What is above
knows what is below, but what is below does not know what is above.
In climbing take careful note of the difficulties along the way;
for as you go up, you can observe them. Coming down you will
no longer see them, but you will know they are there if you have
observed them well. There is an art in finding one's direction
in the lower regions by the memory of what one saw higher up.
When one can no longer see, one can at least know.

RENE DAUMAL

MIKE RITTER

24

<><><><><><><><><><><><><><><><><><><><><><><><><><><><><><><><><>

*Character cannot be developed in ease and quiet.
Only though experiences of trial and suffering can
the soul be strengthened, vision cleared, ambition
inspired and success achieved.*

HELEN KELLER

25

There is a theory which states that if ever anybody
discovers exactly what the universe is for
and why it is here, it will instantly disappear
and be replaced by something even more bizarre
and inexplicable. There is another theory which
states that this has already happened.

DOUGLAS ADAMS

26

*Refusal to believe until proof is given
is a rational position; denial of all
outside of our own limited experience is absurd.*

ANNIE BESANT

27

*Ultimately I have found it is meaningless
to hold the yardstick of fact against the
complexities of the human heart.
Reality simply isn't large enough to hold us.*

A. MANETTE ANSAY

28

✦✦✦✦✦✦✦✦✦✦✦✦✦✦✦✦✦✦✦✦✦✦✦✦✦✦✦✦✦✦

A deep sense of the spiritual leads one to trust not one's own lonely power, but the great flow or pattern manifested in all life, including our own.

RACHEL NAOMI REMEN

29

When a man realizes his littleness —
his greatness can appear.

HERBERT GEORGE WELLS

×◇×◇×◇×◇×◇×◇×◇×◇×◇×◇×◇×◇×◇×◇×◇×◇×◇×◇×

30

The taller the bamboo grows, the lower it bends.

CHINESE PROVERB

MIKE RITTER

31

*We must not cease from exploration
and the end of all our exploring will be
to arrive where we began and
to know the place for the first time.*

T.S. ELIOT

imagination

august

1

The important thing is not to stop questioning.
Curiosity has its own reason for existing.

ALBERT EINSTEIN

2

❖❖❖❖❖❖❖❖❖❖❖❖❖❖❖❖❖❖❖❖❖❖❖❖❖❖❖❖❖❖❖❖

*Literature is where I go to explore the highest
and lowest places in human society
and in the human spirit, where I hope to find not
absolute truth but the truth of the tale,
of the imagination of the heart.*

SALMAN RUSHDIE

3

✕◆◇◆◇◆◇◆◇◆◇◆◇◆◇◆◇◆◇◆◇◆◇◆◇◆◇◆◇◆◇◆◇◆✕

Life is a romantic business.
It is painting a picture, not doing a sum —
but you have to make the romance,
and it will come to the question how much
fire you have in your belly.

OLIVER WENDELL HOLMES

4

✕✕✕✕✕✕✕✕✕✕✕✕✕✕✕✕✕✕✕✕✕✕✕✕✕✕✕✕✕✕✕✕✕✕✕

Since everything is ultimately made out of the same atoms, there's no reason why we can't put them together to create whatever we want.

TSERING DORJEE

ANTONIA MUNROE

5

The whole world is an art gallery
when you're mindful.
There are beautiful things everywhere — and they're free.

CHARLES TART

6

❖❖❖❖❖❖❖❖❖❖❖❖❖❖❖❖❖❖❖❖❖❖❖❖❖❖❖❖❖❖

I know with certainty that a man's work
is nothing but the long journey to recover,
through the detours of art,
the two or three simple and great images
which first gained access to his heart.

ALBERT CAMUS

Abigail Isaacson, Safe Passage volunteer, Bowdoin College '08

Walking to the "campo" (playground), we passed the children's homes. Sandwiched tightly together, the houses were no more than tiny, dirt-floored, tin-roofed, one-room shacks where entire families lived. Despite the cramped space, the dark-interior dwellings housed not only the necessities of a home, such as pots, chairs and often a single bed for an entire family, but they also held the day's work: the discarded materials for which the families had scavenged all day in the dump. Stacks of plastic chairs, for example, lined the side of one house, waiting there until they were sold for recycling. Every inch of these confined areas was used and had a purpose.

Judging from the enthusiastic roar of the kids and the immediate soccer and tag games that began, I gathered we had arrived at the campo. This playground, however, looked nothing like what I was expecting. The slides and play fixtures were hard cement. With broken goal posts at either end, the soccer field was a dust bowl, and there was no grass in sight. The hazy gray that dominated the landscape of the dump permeated the playground as well.

My memory of the houses we passed that day and the hard, grubby playground stands in stark contrast to the beautiful new building I encountered when I returned the next year. Freshly painted yellow and white, the Safe Passage Center is located a few blocks up the hill from the entrance to the dump, farther away from the loud passing trucks and the billows of dust from the streets. Although the smell of trash remains ever-present, the air inside the new school feels cleaner. All of the fixtures are new; there are working bathrooms with running toilets and sinks, and the classrooms are bright, spacious and organized. In the center of the building, a small courtyard and flower garden are exposed to the sky through an open roof.

When I first saw the new building, it struck me as incongruous to have such a beautiful center in such a filthy dump. The little bit of green in the center of this new courtyard was perhaps the only grass I had seen. In an area so laden by dust, covered in brown, reeking of trash, and pressed for space, this small patch of rich, healthy, emerald grass continues to strike me. The opportunity to know a peaceful space, uncluttered by the necessities of life, where plants grow simply for their beauty strikes me as an experience every child deserves. Just as reading and writing improve these children's present existence, so too a few blades of grass enhance the confined space in which they live, while at the same time enriching their image of the broader world.

7

◇◇

The chief business of my life has always been to indulge my senses; I never knew anything of greater importance.

GIACOMO CASANOVA DE SEINGALT

8

There are two lasting bequests we can give our children:
One is roots. The other is wings.

HODDING CARTER JR.

MIKE RITTER

MIKE RITTER

9

Children laugh, on average, up to 300 times a day, adults just 17.

DANIEL NETTLE

❖❖❖❖❖❖❖❖❖❖❖❖❖❖❖❖❖❖❖❖❖❖❖❖❖❖❖❖❖❖❖

10

All kids need a little help, a little hope and somebody who believes in them.

EARVIN 'MAGIC' JOHNSON

11

*You will never stand taller than when you kneel
to help a child.*

AUTHOR UNKNOWN

12

International Youth Day

✕✕✕

*Why, sometimes I've believed as many as
six impossible things before breakfast.*

LEWIS CARROLL

13

*If my heart can become pure and simple
like that of a child, I think there probably can be
no greater happiness than this.*

KITARO NISHIDA

14

Every child, and the child in every one of us,
is ready to plead: Tell me a story.
For the role of stories is to explain life, and the good
stories, in their very substance and in the structure
of their language, become revelation.

ANDREW GREELEY

15

The further you progress, the more you will perceive that the universe is divine.

ARNAUD DESJARDINS

◇◇◇◇◇◇◇◇◇◇◇◇◇◇◇◇◇◇◇◇◇◇◇◇◇◇◇◇◇◇◇◇◇◇◇◇◇

16

All that I have seen teaches me to trust the Creator for all I have not seen.

RALPH WALDO EMERSON

JON TORRES

17

❖❖❖❖❖❖❖❖❖❖❖❖❖❖❖❖❖❖❖❖❖❖❖❖

In this my green world
Flowers birds are hands
They hold me
I am loved all day
All this pleases me
I am amused
I have to laugh from crying
Trees mountains are arms
I am loved all day.

KENNETH PATCHEN

18

<svg>border decoration</svg>

I will make you brooches & toys for your delight
Of bird-song at morning & star-shine at night
I will make you a palace fit for you & me
Of green days in forests & blue days at sea.

ROBERT LOUIS STEVENSON

19

*It is not the critic who counts; not the man
who points out how the strong man stumbles,
or where the doer of deeds could have
done them better. The credit belongs to the
man who is actually in the arena, whose face
is marred by dust and sweat and blood.*

THEODORE ROOSEVELT

20

*Flowers leave some of their fragrance
in the hand that bestows them.*

CHINESE PROVERB

21

✕◇◇◇◇◇◇◇◇◇◇◇◇◇◇◇◇◇◇◇◇◇◇◇◇◇◇◇◇◇◇◇✕

*It is one of the commonest of mistakes to consider
that the limit of perception is also the limit
of all there is to perceive.*

C.W. LEADBETTER

22

*It all depends on how we look at things
and not on how they are in themselves.*

CARL JUNG

◇◇

23

*Even a midget standing on the shoulders
of a giant will always see further.*

VIKTOR FRANKL

24

✕◇◇◇◇◇◇◇◇◇◇◇◇◇◇◇◇◇◇◇◇◇◇◇◇◇◇◇◇◇◇◇◇✕

You write about my flower as if I think and see what you think and see of the flower, and I don't.

Georgia O'Keeffe

25

Better keep yourself clean and bright; you are the window through which you must see the world.

GEORGE BERNARD SHAW

26

✕✕✕✕✕✕✕✕✕✕✕✕✕✕✕✕✕✕✕✕✕✕✕✕✕✕✕✕✕✕✕✕✕✕✕✕

It is only with the heart that one can see rightly;
what is essential is invisible to the eye.

ANTOINE DE SAINT-EXUPÉRY

27

In my prints I try to show that we live
in a beautiful and orderly world and not in a chaos
without norms, as we sometimes seem to.

M.C. ESCHER

28

✕◇✕◇✕◇✕◇✕◇✕◇✕◇✕◇✕◇✕◇✕◇✕◇✕◇✕◇✕◇✕◇✕◇✕◇✕

I tell you, don't let your hearts grow numb.
Stay alert.
It is your soul that matters.

ALBERT SCHWEITZER

29

Though we are different, we were born involved in one another.

T'AO CH'IEN

✦✦✦✦✦✦✦✦✦✦✦✦✦✦✦✦✦✦✦✦✦✦✦✦✦✦✦✦✦✦✦

30

*Spend time every day listening
To what your muse is trying to tell you.*

SAINT BARTHOLOMEW

JOSEPH DELCONZO

31

Only in quiet waters do things mirror themselves distorted. Only in a quiet mind is adequate perception of the world.

HANS MARGOLIUS

change

september

1

❖❖❖❖❖❖❖❖❖❖❖❖❖❖❖❖❖❖❖❖❖❖❖❖❖❖❖❖❖❖❖❖

Where there is hope there is life,
where there is life there is possibility,
and where there is possibility change can occur.

THE REV. JESSE JACKSON

JOHN SANTERRE

2

*Everything in life that we really accept
undergoes a change.*

KATHERINE MANSFIELD

3

The first step toward change is acceptance....
Change is not something you do, it's something you allow.

WILL GARCIA

4

✕◇✕

My old father used to have a saying:
If you make a bad bargain, hug it all the tighter.

ABRAHAM LINCOLN

5

◇◇◇◇◇◇◇◇◇◇◇◇◇◇◇◇◇◇◇◇◇◇◇◇◇◇◇◇◇◇◇◇◇◇

*All changes, even the most longed for,
have their melancholy; for what we leave behind us
is a part of ourselves; we must die to one life before
we can enter another.*

ANATOLE FRANCE

6

◇◇◇◇◇◇◇◇◇◇◇◇◇◇◇◇◇◇◇◇◇◇◇◇◇◇◇◇◇◇◇◇◇◇◇◇◇◇

Time as he grows old teaches many lessons.

AESCHYLUS

7

They always say time changes things,
but you actually have to change them yourself.

ANDY WARHOL

8

<><><><><><><><><><><><><><><><><><><><><><><><><><><><><><>

The healthy being craves an occasional wildness,
a jolt from normality, a sharpening of the edge
of appetite, his own little festival of the Saturnalia,
a brief excursion from his way of life.

ROBERT MacIVER

9

✕◇◇◇◇◇◇◇◇◇◇◇◇◇◇◇◇◇◇◇◇◇◇◇◇◇◇◇◇◇◇◇✕

Everyone wants to feel more interesting,
but that's the curiosity of knowing someone,
finding out things about them, letting them open
up to you. It's beautiful. Change happens when
you've forgotten about it.

KARNA SOUTHALL

10

You can't be neurotic in front of a bunch of trees.

THOMAS MERTON

◇◇

11

The circumstances of the world are so variable that an irrevocable purpose or opinion is almost synonymous with a foolish one.

WILLIAM H. SEWARD

MIKE RITTER

12

✕✕✕

In times of profound change,
the learners inherit the earth, while the learned
find themselves beautifully equipped
to deal with a world that no longer exists.

ERIC HOFFER

13

*I wish more people would share the ways
of their grandmothers. I think it would help
the present world situation if we all learned to value
and respect the way of the grandmothers —
our own as well as everyone else's.*

BEVERLY HUNGRY WOLF

14

*Excellence is the best deterrent
to racism and sexism.*

Oprah Winfrey

✕◇✕

15

*Humanity will thrive when the world
appreciates the value of diversity.*

Indira Gandhi

16

✕◇◆◇◆◇◆◇◆◇◆◇◆◇◆◇◆◇◆◇◆◇◆◇◆◇◆◇◆◇◆◇◆◇◆◇◆◇✕

You must not lose faith in humanity.
Humanity is an ocean; if a few drops of the ocean
are dirty, the ocean does not become dirty.

GANDHI

17

The good we secure for ourselves is precarious
and uncertain until it is secured for all of us
and incorporated into our common life.

JANE ADDAMS

18

✧✧✧✧✧✧✧✧✧✧✧✧✧✧✧✧✧✧✧✧✧✧✧✧✧✧✧✧✧✧✧✧✧

Peace is not the absence of anything.
Real peace is the presence of something beautiful.
Both peace and the thirst for it have been
in the heart of every human being in every century
and every civilization.

MAHARAJI

19

◇◇◇◇◇◇◇◇◇◇◇◇◇◇◇◇◇◇◇◇◇◇◇◇◇◇◇◇◇◇◇◇◇◇◇◇

Peace is not merely an absence of war.
It is also a state of mind. Lasting peace can come
only to peaceful people.

JAWAHARLAL NEHRU

20

✕✕✕✕✕✕✕✕✕✕✕✕✕✕✕✕✕✕✕✕✕✕✕✕✕✕✕✕✕✕

If in our daily life we can smile,
if we can be peaceful and happy, not only we,
but everyone will profit from it.
This is the most basic kind of peace work.

THICH NHAT HANH

JOHN SANTERRE

21

International Day of Peace

If we have no peace, it is because we have forgotten that we belong to each other.

MOTHER TERESA

22

*If powerful men and women could center themselves
in it, the whole world would be transformed by itself,
in its natural rhythms. People would be content
with their simple everyday lives, in harmony,
and free of desire. When there is no desire,
all things are at peace.*

Tao Te Ching

Dorien Claessen, Safe Passage and La Luna volunteer

From "Are Vultures Birds, or Not?"

Juan is eight years old. He has a twin brother who lives with his mother in the capital city. Juan, on the other hand, resides in the living community, as his mother cannot take care of all her children at the same time. Juan and I make a picture with chalk on the painter's easel. Juan asks me to draw a house, as he draws the clouds. We both write down all the names of the people in the house. Juan asks me to write down my name and his name on the side of the house. And this is how it happens.

"Those are pretty clouds you drew. Are these birds?" I ask.

"No," Juan says. "Vultures."

23

Deep peace of the running waves to you.
Deep peace of the flowing air to you.
Deep peace of the shining stars to you.
Deep peace of the quiet earth to you.
Deep peace of the infinite peace to you.

GAELIC PRAYER

24

If you are patient in one moment of anger, you will escape a hundred days of sorrow.

CHINESE PROVERB

Mary Herman, Maine's former first lady
Former Safe Passage board member:
Volunteer with "Guatemalax"

In July of 2006, I was fortunate to lead 10 Brunswick (Maine) lacrosse players on a 10-day service trip to Safe Passage. I remember vividly Hanley meeting us as we arrived Monday morning at the Guardería (Early Intervention and Day Care Center). She hugged me and I cried with joy that we were finally THERE! As Hanley gave us an in-depth tour of the entire project, she told us the story of her first visit to the neighborhood around the dump. When she first was taken to see the dump, she said, "This can't be." To me these words resonate daily; to me they mean both "I cannot believe that people must live this way" AND "This cannot continue."

25

Most of us have spent our lives caught up in plans,
expectations, ambitions for the future,
in regrets, guilt or shame about the past.
To come into the present is to stop the war.

JACK KORNFIELD

26

Though we travel the world over to find the beautiful, we must carry it with us or we find it not.

RALPH WALDO EMERSON

✕◇✕

27

A feeling of warmth creates a kind of openness. You'll find that all human beings are just like you.

THE 14TH DALAI LAMA

DANIELLE TORRES

28

◇◇◇◇◇◇◇◇◇◇◇◇◇◇◇◇◇◇◇◇◇◇◇◇◇◇◇◇◇◇◇◇◇◇◇◇◇◇

Everything that has a beginning has an ending.
Make your peace with that and all will be well.

BUDDHA

29

Know thyself.

SOCRATES

30

Feeling light within,
I walk.

NAVAJO INDIAN CHANT

326

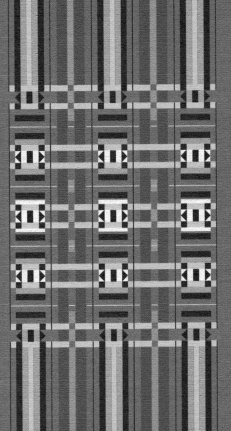

opportunity

october

1

Chance favors the prepared mind.

Louis Pasteur

2

The past may become either an opportunity or an obstacle. Everything depends on what we make of it and not what it makes of us.

Sarvepalli Radhakrishnan

3

Whether talking about individuals or governments,
the principle that must guide us is that of human rights.
If we live in a country where human rights exist
and are respected, we are naturally responsible
for our duties and responsibilities.

THE 14TH DALAI LAMA

4

*I'm a great believer in luck, and I find the harder
I work, the more I have of it.*

THOMAS JEFFERSON

5

*People always call it luck when you've acted
more sensibly than they have.*

ANNE TYLER

6

Every successful person I have heard of has done the best he could with the conditions as he found them, and not waited until next year for better.

E.W. HOWE

JOSEPH DELCONZO

7

*People become really quite remarkable
when they start thinking that they can do things.
When they believe in themselves
they have the first secret of success.*

NORMAN VINCENT PEALE

8

Keep away from people who try to belittle your
ambitions. Small people always do that,
but the really great make you feel
that you, too, can become great.

MARK TWAIN

9

To laugh often and much; to win the respect of
intelligent people and the affection of children;...
to leave the world a bit better, whether by
a healthy child, a garden patch or a redeemed
social condition; to know even one life
has breathed easier because you have lived.
This is to have succeeded.

RALPH WALDO EMERSON

10

*For success, like happiness, cannot be pursued;
it must ensue, and it only does so as the unintended
side effect of one's personal dedication to a cause
greater than oneself.*

VIKTOR FRANKL

11

*Grandmother says daylight is wiser than the dark.
Let us sleep now and plan tomorrow.*

Ishi, Last of the Yahi Tribe

Ali Totta, high school student and volunteer

While I am only 14, Safe Passage is already an important part of my life. The children attending this program are in my thoughts daily — especially the two children that my family sponsors, Monica and Immer. Our first lunch together was at Burger King. Immer ordered a burger and after every bite he would wrap his burger up, eat a few fries, take a sip of his orange soda, and then unwrap his burger again. It was only his second time out of the dump area, and I could tell he wanted to savor it. Immer was sitting closest to the Burger King crowns, and he decided to try one of them on. In his efforts to find a bigger one, he placed a few different crowns on his head until we realized what he was searching for and showed him how to adjust the size. Monica followed after Immer and wore a crown, too. The two of them didn't remove their crowns for the rest of the outing....

Lucinda Dickens Hawksley

From the Dickens Oration
London, England, Sunday, June 3, 2007

Although at times it was heartbreaking, my time in Guatemala was also one of great excitement as there are so many wonderful charities working out there. I met large numbers of people who are tirelessly devoting their whole lives to helping the poor and disenfranchised. I also finally met the child I have been sponsoring in Guatemala for the last six years, a lovely little boy called Alex, whose entire village turned out to greet me and welcome me into their home. I was deeply humbled by witnessing the incredible difference that my paltry £16 a month has made to an entire community. Alex and his three siblings all go to school, the family has clean water (which I am living proof of as they gave me salad for lunch!) and his family are happily making their way in life after the decades of war, together. Alex's older brother is also training as a runner: It's my hope that he will end up representing Guatemala in the 2012 Olympics in London.

12

Success is a... trendy word.
Don't aim for success if you want it;
just do what you love and it will come naturally.

DAVID FROST

13

You've achieved success in your field when you don't know whether what you are doing is work or play.

WARREN BEATTY

14

*One could do worse
Than be a swinger of birches.*

ROBERT FROST

15

*That some good can be derived from every event
is a better proposition than that everything happens
for the best, which it assuredly does not.*

JAMES FEIBLEMAN

16

How can they say my life is not a success?
Have I not for more than 60 years got enough
to eat and escaped being eaten?

LOGAN SMITH

17

When one door closes, another door opens;
but we often look so long and so regretfully
upon the closed door that we do not see
the ones which open for us.

ALEXANDER GRAHAM BELL

MIKE RITTER

18

Half the failures in life arise from pulling in one's horse as he is leaping.

JULIUS HARE

19

Mistakes are portals of discovery.

JAMES JOYCE

20

The person who makes no mistakes
usually never makes anything.

Bishop William Magee

21

I have not failed. I have successfully found
10,000 ways that will not work.

Thomas Edison

22

*Setbacks in trying to realize the ideal
do not prove that the ideal is at fault.*

DAG HAMMARSKJOLD

23

*We need to make the kind of society
where it is easier for people to be good.*

PETER MAUPIN

24

United Nations Day

Within a system which denies the existence of basic human rights,
fear tends to be the order of the day....
A most insidious form of fear is that which masquerades
as common sense or even wisdom, condemning as foolish, reckless,
insignificant or futile the small, daily acts of courage
which held to preserve man's self respect
and inherent human dignity.

AUNG SAN SUU KYI

25

*We must understand the role of human rights
as empowering of individuals and communities.
By protecting these rights, we can help prevent the
many conflicts based on poverty, discrimination
and exclusion (social, economic and political)
that continue to plague humanity.*

MARY ROBINSON

26

We may have different religions, different languages,
different colored skin,
but we all belong to one human race.
We all share the same basic values.

Kofi Annan

27

*The poor themselves can create a poverty-free world —
all we have to do is to free them from the chains
that we have put around them.*

MUHAMMAD YUNUS

28

*Opportunity is missed by most people
because it is dressed in overalls and looks like work.*

THOMAS EDISON

29

*Since patience or tolerance comes from an ability
to remain firm and steadfast and not be overwhelmed
by the adverse situations or conditions that one faces,
one should not see tolerance or patience as a kind
of weakness, or giving in, but rather as a sign of strength,
coming from a deep ability to remain firm.*

THE 14TH DALAI LAMA

MIKE RITTER

30

A society grows great when old men plant trees whose shade they know they shall never sit in.

GREEK PROVERB

31

Halloween

*An idea, like a ghost, must be spoken
a little before it will explain itself.*

CHARLES DICKENS

gratitude

november

1

All Saints Day

People do not die for us immediately,
but remain bathed in a sort of aura of life
which bears no relation to true immortality but
through which they continue to occupy our thoughts
in the same way as when they were alive.
It is as though they were traveling abroad.

MARCEL PROUST

MIKE RITTER

2

All Souls Day

*Mayhap a funeral among men
is a wedding among the angels.*

Kahlil Gibran

3

When everything else has gone from my brain — the president's name, the state capitals, the neighborhoods where I lived and then my own name, and what it was on earth I sought, and then at length the faces of my friends, and finally the faces of my family — when all this has dissolved, what will be left, I believe, is topology: the dreaming memory of land as it lay this way and that.

ANNIE DILLARD

4

*I do not want to die… until I have
faithfully made the most of my talent
and cultivated the seed that was placed in me
until the last small twig has gone.*

KATHE KOLLWITZ

5

*Our Creator would never have given us
such lovely days —
and given us the deep hearts to enjoy them —
unless we were meant to be immortal.*

NATHANIEL HAWTHORNE

6

Love makes people believe in immortality because there seems not to be room enough in life for so great a tenderness and it is inconceivable that the most masterful of our emotions should have no more than the spare moments of a few brief years.

ROBERT LOUIS STEVENSON

7

But listen to me; for one moment,
Quit being sad.
Hear blessings dropping their blossoms around you.

RUMI

8

Don't we in praise somehow enjoy what we praise,
however far we are from it?

C.S. LEWIS

9

I thank you God for most this amazing day:
for the leaping greenly spirits of trees
and a blue true dream of sky; and for everything
which is natural which is infinite which is yes.

E.E. CUMMINGS

10

Nothing is worth more than this day.

JOHANN WOLFGANG VON GOETHE

11

Veterans Day

We are all in the same boat on a stormy sea,
and we owe each other a terrible loyalty.

GILBERT KEITH CHESTERTON

12

It is completely usual for me to get up in the morning, take a look around, and laugh out loud.

BARBARA KINGSOLVER

13

The way to start a day is this —
Go outside and face the east and greet the sun with
some kind of blessing or chant or song that you made
yourself and keep for early morning.

BYRD BAYLOR

MIKE RITTER

14

Sometimes it's better to rise up
out of the ashes, singing.

JANE YOLEN

15

You are amazing grace.
You are a precious jewel —
You — special, miraculous, unrepeatable, fragile,
fearful, tender, lost, sparkling
ruby emerald jewel rainbow splendor person.
You are amazing grace.

Joan Baez

Amina LaCour

From "Notes from the Early Childhood Program"

"Questions, doubts or comments anyone would like to share?" I shouted over the loud grinding noise coming from the plastic recycling machine next door. It was Tuesday afternoon, and we were finishing our weekly planning meeting with staff and volunteers in the "old guardería." The children had left over an hour ago. Today was a good day: All the children had been picked up on time, and it wasn't raining – yet. Sonia, our cleaner and cook, was bustling around between the kitchen and the pila (Guatemalan outdoor sink) in the back of the guardería. The heat was stifling, the flies were buzzing, and there was the usual stench that one grows accustomed to. Suddenly one of the teachers let out a stifled shriek, "Allí va otra..." or "There goes another one..." Everyone turned and cringed as a rat scurried along the wall heading toward one of the many cracks and holes between the lamina. A peal of laughter erupted as one of the volunteers jumped up and tried to balance on the rickety plastic stool she was sitting on.

Sonia came running from the kitchen armed with a squirt bottle of chlorine solution (like most animals, rats don't like the smell of chlorine). After the mixture of laughter and groans from teachers and volunteers died down, everyone seated themselves again – some with their feet raised off the floor. I apologized, reminding everyone that we would be moving into a new building soon. In our current situation we simply had no way of sealing all the holes in the warehouse that we were temporarily in, and there was no way that we could rid ourselves of the rat population that was breeding outside. The best we could do was to keep them at bay. The noise and bustle of the children combined with daily routine chlorine sprays usually kept most of the rats away during the day. However, telltale signs each morning let us know that our area in the warehouse was one of the most popular nightly party spots for local rats.

Despite the rats, the heat, the noise, the stench and the flies, we did have running water, toilets, and – above all – a safe place where the teachers, volunteers and children kept coming, with much dedication, love and hope. And they continue to come today, with the same dedication, love, and hope – but now to a wonderful new facility. A facility with windows that let in the sunlight, walls with no cracks or holes, and brand new furniture and toys. A kitchen that is always well stocked, and gardens where flowers and grass thrive. A facility that inspires even more joy, love and learning. Things that I have not grown accustomed to yet, and hopefully never will.

Safe Passage – and Hanley – has and always will be a constant reminder for me to appreciate every moment and be grateful for even the simplest of things, in some sense even the rats. The rats that served us all as a compelling force to create a new facility for the early childhood program. The rats that now serve to remind us of how things were, and how they continue to be in the homes of the children with whom we work.

16

You are your most valuable asset. Don't forget that.
You are the best thing you have.

Gary Paulsen

17

*Establishing self-pride among the young
is one of the most important goals.
It's hard to be productive
if you don't have pride in what you are.*

CLIFF ALLEN

18

Be yourself. Everyone else is already taken.

OSCAR WILDE

19

Were it not for the way you taught me to look at the world, to see the life at play in everything, I would be lonely forever.

TED KOOSER

JOHN SANTERRE

20

Me, myself, I consider us lucky.
We are very lucky to have this dump here.
It doesn't make me feel sorry for myself.
It doesn't make me think bad about myself,
because at least I'm working honestly.
We're all human. We all have eyes to see
and a heart to feel.

CHARLIE DE LEON FROM *RECYCLED LIFE*

21

You make a living by what you get.
You make a life by what you give.

WINSTON CHURCHILL

22

Gratitude is not only the greatest virtue,
but the parent to all the others.

CICERO

I give you this one thought to keep:
I am with you still, I do not sleep.
I am a thousand winds that blow,
I am the diamond glints in snow,
I am the sunlight on ripened grain,
I am the gentle autumn rain.
When you awaken in the morning's hush,
I am the swift uplifting rush
Of quiet birds in circled flight.
I am the soft stars that shine at night.
Do not think of me as gone.
I am with you still — in each new dawn.

NATIVE AMERICAN PRAYER

24

*In daily life we must see that it is
not happiness that makes us grateful,
but gratefulness that makes us happy.*

DAVID STEINDL-RAST

25

*My piece of bread only belongs to me
when I know that everyone else has a share,
and that no one starves while I eat.*

LEO TOLSTOY

26

*Gardening is an active participation
in the deepest mysteries of the universe.*

THOMAS BERRY

27

Prosperity is the outpouring of substance in all our affairs.
Everything in the universe is for us.
Nothing is against us. Life is giving of itself.

ERNEST HOLMES

28

For everything there is a season
and a time for every purpose under heaven
a time to be born, and a time to die,
a time to plant and a time to pluck
what is planted...

ECCLESIASTES 3:1-2

29

With every deed you are sowing a seed,
though the harvest you may not see.

ELLA WHEELER WILCOX

30

*Let us be grateful to people who make us happy;
they are the charming gardeners
who make our souls blossom.*

Marcel Proust

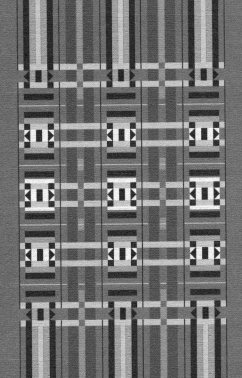

reflection

december

1

*One of the greatest feelings in life is the conviction
that you have lived the life you wanted to live —
with the rough and the smooth,
the good and the bad — but yours,
shaped by your own choices, and not someone else's.*

MICHAEL IGNATIEFF

2

This is the true joy in life, the being used for a purpose recognized by yourself as a mighty one; the being thoroughly worn out before you are thrown on the scrap heap; the being a force of nature instead of a feverish, selfish, little clod of ailments and grievances complaining that the world will not devote itself to making you happy.

GEORGE BERNARD SHAW

ANTONIA MUNROE

3

*And did you get what
you wanted from this life, even so?
I did.
And what did you want?
To call myself beloved, to feel myself
beloved on the earth.*

Raymond Carver

4

*When I was a child, I learned that
the moon was the goddess Dewi Ratih.
Then Neil Armstrong landed on it.
I still look up at night and pray to Dewi Ratih.*

SURADNYA

5

Nothing is really impossible if you know how to control the mind. In the cold you can remain warm, and in the heat stay cool. You can communicate over great distances, and I will teach you how not to feel tired when walking. Would you like to walk so fast that you almost fly?

GEWA KARMAPA LAMA

6

Where there is great love, there are always miracles.

Willa Cather

7

Everything is miraculous. It is miraculous that one does not melt in one's bath.

Pablo Picasso

8

*We must not allow the clock and the calendar
to blind us to the fact that each moment of life
is a miracle and mystery.*

H.G. WELLS

*Happiness is a mystery like religion,
and it should never be rationalized.*

GILBERT KEITH CHESTERTON

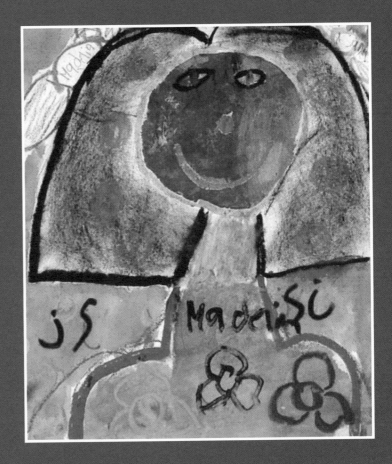

10

When a lot of things start going wrong all at once,
it is to protect something big and lovely
that is trying to get itself born — and that
this something needs for you to be distracted
so that it can be born as perfectly as possible.

ANNE LAMOTT

11

At a certain point, life has no more secrets to reveal.
You live as if there is one reality,
and in return it pays you richly.

DEEPAK CHOPRA

12

Once we conclude that the basic nature of humanity is compassionate rather than aggressive, our relationship to the world around us changes immediately. Seeing others as basically compassionate instead of hostile and selfish helps us relax, trust, live at ease. It makes us happier.

HOWARD CUTLER

JOHN SANTERRE

13

I am a kind of paranoiac in reverse.
I suspect people of plotting to make me happy.

J.D. Salinger

14

The secret to contentment is knowing
how to enjoy what you have, and be able to lose
all desire for things beyond your reach.

Lin Yutang

15

This is happiness: to be dissolved into something complete and great.

WILLA CATHER

16

*When you reach the heart of life, you shall find
beauty in all things, even in the eyes
that are blind to beauty.*

KAHLIL GIBRAN

17

Be as a bird perched on a frail branch
that she feels bending beneath her,
still she sings away all the same,
knowing she has wings.

VICTOR HUGO

MIKE RITTER

18

*Happiness is not in our circumstances,
but in ourselves. It is not something we see,
like a rainbow, or feel, like the heat of a fire.
Happiness is something we are.*

JOHN B. SHEERIN

19

Some of the briefest moments capture us,
force us to take them in, and demand that we
live the rest of our lives in reference to them.

LUCY GREALY

20

*A thought, even a possibility, can shatter us
and transform us.*

FRIEDRICH NIETZSCHE

21

Sometimes you get tempted to make something wonderful even better, but in doing so you lose what was so wonderful to begin with.

POLLY HORVATH

22

*True nobility is not about
being better than someone else;
rather, it's about being better
than you used to be.*

Dr. Wayne W. Dyer

23

There is an old Chinese belief that when the baby begins to smile he is becoming a person. That smile is telling for it reveals a sense of self and a feeling of well-being and intactness.

GEZA ROHEIM

24

Choose life! Only that and always!
And at whatever risk, to let life leak out,
to let it wear away by the mere passage of time,
to withhold giving it
and spreading it is to choose nothing.

SR. HELEN KELLY

25

Christmas

To live is the rarest thing in the world.
Most people exist, that is all.

OSCAR WILDE

26

The greatest revolution of our generation
is the discovery that human beings,
by changing the inner attitudes of their minds,
can change the outer aspects of their lives.

WILLIAM JAMES

27

*The most powerful thing you can do
to change the world, is to change your own beliefs
about the nature of life, people, reality,
to something more positive.*

SHAKTI GAWAIN

Becky Pride, Safe Passage volunteer

Hanley was the most innocent, joyous, tirelessly enthusiastic person I have known in my 57 years. She was also smart, savvy, intellectually keen, motivationally astute — a virtual mover of mountains. She was egoless and yet a powerful force with whom to be reckoned. She wanted the best for all human beings. She made each of us — no matter our shortcomings or foibles — feel appreciated, loved and encouraged. No gift of our time, talent, finance was too insignificant; no little triumph was ever minimized. She was thrilled for each gift, each action. Our attempts — no matter how feeble from our own points of view — were celebrated by her as superhuman feats.

Our joy made her joyous.

To have Hanley for 36 years was a priceless gift. She showed us the way to know joy, freedom, light and love. She modeled the paths of service, sacrifice, commitment, and by so doing, showed us how to experience profound meaning, true happiness and abundant love. Paradoxically, by giving all that she was and all that she had, she drew all the world to her and made the world a far better place.

If we choose to do so, we can know that joy and that peace that passes all understanding.

Hanley's life was as fleetingly fast and brilliant as a meteor, and her impact will not lessen as the years continue to unfold.

28

It is good to have an end to journey towards,
but it is the journey that matters in the end.

URSULA K. LE GUIN

29

We turn not older with the years, but new every day.

EMILY DICKINSON

30

I do not know what I may appear to the world;
but to myself I seem to have been only like a boy
playing on the seashore, and diverting myself
in now and then finding a smoother pebble
or a prettier shell than ordinary, whilst the great
ocean of truth lay all undiscovered before me.

ISAAC NEWTON

31

*In the midst of winter,
I learned that there was within me
an invincible summer.*

ALBERT CAMUS

gratitude &
giving

our daily tread acknowledgments:
sharing what we have

our daily tread began with a birthday celebration.

It was January 19, 2007. Busy with party preparations, we heard the kitchen door slam as our 13-year-old returned from basketball practice. He called out: "Hey Mom and Dad! You know the person who founded Safe Passage? The one you went to college with? They told us in school – she was killed in a car accident yesterday."

I thought I must not have heard him correctly. Hanley was only 36, my age as of that day. Unfortunately, it was true. Hanley Denning, the woman known as *"El Angel del Basurero,"* or "The Angel of the Garbage Dump," had died on January 18. Her family and friends were gathering to mourn even as mine were gathering to celebrate.

I thought about Hanley as I greeted my birthday guests. I had intended to contact my college classmate and find out how I might support her efforts in Guatemala. Caught up in the demands of parenthood and medical training, I had not done so.

I considered what she might have told me. Based on what I knew of her work with Safe Passage, it seemed she might have shared the words of our fellow Bowdoin College graduate Henry Wadsworth Longfellow: "Give what you have. To someone else it may be better than you dare to think." The question was: What did I have to give?

The answer came from Debra, one of my birthday-party friends (and high school classmate). She suggested we create a book. Called **our daily tread**, the book would consist of a year's worth of quotes to contemplate while running, walking and going about the process of living. In addition to raising money for Safe Passage, it would serve to honor Hanley, an elite runner and athlete.

As a fellow runner, writer and lifelong quote collector, I felt that **our daily tread** would be an ideal way for me to contribute to Safe Passage. Except...I still had a medical practice, three children and a husband. The minutes of each day seemed spirited away, always just beyond my grasp. Then help arrived.

Help arrived in the form of Jane Gallagher, Marina Denning and Paul Sutherland. These were people who were dedicated to Safe Passage: people who knew and loved Hanley. More importantly, these were individuals who could get things done. Soon, we were receiving quotes, pictures, artwork and essays from around the world. Not long after, one of my high school classmates, Bonnie Hamalainen, joined our efforts, as the designer and art director of **our daily tread**. My remarkable friend had never even met Hanley; she just simply decided to "give what she had." I am deeply grateful to Bonnie, Jane, Marina and Paul.

I am also grateful to my husband, Kevin Haley, and children, Campbell, Abby and Sophie, who gave me the time, space and support to bring this project to completion.

Many others have given to this project and are deserving of thanks. They include: Angela Raven (project manager), Dean Lunt (publishing consultant), Elizabeth Kistler (summer intern), Jon Torres (photography coordinator), Kristen Funkhouser Pierce (artwork coordinator), Becky Pride (essay and content editor), Kat Gillies and Antonia Munroe (children's art gatherers), Kate Pietropaoli (marketing and distribution coordinator), Rob Landry (website designer), Mary Sunshine (fund-raising consultant), Elizabeth Horton (marketing consultant), Mike Denning (steering committee member), Jordan Denning, Margaret Samuelson, Christina Pulkinen, Mardi Link, Rachel Meyn, Doug Pride, Abby Belisle Haley, Alex Trippe, Alex Finkle, Charlotte Agell, Rich Smith, Debra Friedrich, Christine Slater, Laurie Totta, Kate Mather, Kathy Dall, all of the **ODT** essay writers, artists, and photographers Joseph Delconzo, Mike Glad, Antonia Munroe,

Mike Ritter, John Santerre, Jon Torres, and Danielle Torres — each of whom donated photography previously to Safe Passage and generously contributed their work once again for inclusion in this book.

Also, thanks to quote contributors from around the world, especially those from Harrison Middle School, Yarmouth High School and the Maine Track Club. Finally, thank you to Bowdoin College, Wheelock College, Islandport Press and all of the individuals I have not the space to name (or may have inadvertently forgotten).

Whenever something was lacking, someone stepped in, sharing both joyfully and deliberately.

It was as if an angel were watching over the process, willing us to succeed: an angel born one January day.

Lisa M. Belisle, M.D., M.P.H.
October 2008

JOHN SANTERRE

sharing what you have
and who you are

Thank you for being a part of **our daily tread**. By purchasing this book, you have shared what you have with the children of Safe Passage.

We hope you have been inspired as you have traveled these pages, pondering passages and enjoying the scenery along the way. We hope you have journeyed deliberately and with joy. Now it is time to take action: It is time to share who you are.

You do not have to be a teacher or a runner. You do not have to found an organization that benefits Guatemalan children. You simply need to have the desire to share your interests, skills or love.

You may learn more about sharing with Safe Passage by visiting www.safepassage.org. You may learn about sharing with other organizations by visiting www.wiserearth.org. For other ideas, or to let us know how you are sharing with others, visit www.dailytread.com.

Thank you for sharing what you have and who you are.
May you live your life deliberately, and with joy.

~LB

JOHN SANTERRE

Hanley Denning
on the essentials of leadership

First, have a vision, and never lose sight of it.
Second, be patient and extremely disciplined.
Third, embrace and listen to those around you.
Fourth, be a hands-on worker and leader.
Fifth, be willing to make mistakes and take risks.
Sixth, persistence is a must — don't give up.

from a talk at Maine's Institute of Civic Leadership

COLOPHON

This book was typeset in OpenType versions of fonts Perpetua Roman and Italic and the type family Myriad Pro. Perpetua was originally designed by Eric Gill for the Monotype Corp. between 1925 and 1932. Myriad Pro was designed by Robert Slimbach and Carol Twombly with Fred Brady and Christopher Slye in 1992 for Adobe.

ABOUT THE DESIGN This book is comprised of myriad elements, or threads: the story of Hanley Denning and Safe Passage, monthly themes, daily quotes, documentary photography and children's artwork. Introductory chapter illustrations — contemporary interpretations of native Guatemalan tapestries and fiber arts — weave these threads together.